Cadassses
tacc
ip 8/89
+Bind
Duraflex

Headline Series

No. 289   FOREIGN POLICY ASSOCIATION   Summer 1989

Women, Poverty and Progress in the Third World

by Mayra Buvinić and Sally W. Yudelman

Cover Design: Ed Bohon $4.00
UN Photo/Doranne Jacobson

The Authors

MAYRA BUVINIĆ, director and a founding member of the International Center for Research on Women (ICRW) in Washington, D.C., is a trustee of the International Institute of Tropical Agriculture and a member of the Overseas Development Council's Program Advisory Committee. Dr. Buvinić is the author of numerous works on the poverty of women in developing countries.

SALLY W. YUDELMAN, a senior fellow at the ICRW, worked from 1972 to 1984 at the Inter-American Foundation, where she became the first woman vice-president. A Woodrow Wilson visiting fellow, she served this past year on the International Commission for Central American Recovery and Development and has written extensively about nongovernmental organizations and women's issues.

The Foreign Policy Association

The Foreign Policy Association is a private, nonprofit, nonpartisan educational organization. Its purpose is to stimulate wider interest and more effective participation in, and greater understanding of, world affairs among American citizens. Among its activities is the continuous publication, dating from 1935, of the HEADLINE SERIES.

The International Center for Research on Women

The ICRW is a nonprofit organization established in 1976 to increase women's economic participation in developing countries in order to fight poverty, reduce inequities, and promote economic growth, through research, technical assistance, public education, and public information programs.

HEADLINE SERIES (ISSN 0017-8780) is published four times a year, Winter, Spring, Summer and Fall, by the Foreign Policy Association, Inc., 729 Seventh Ave., New York, N.Y. 10019. Chairman, Robert V. Lindsay; President, John W. Kiermaier; Editor in Chief, Nancy L. Hoepli; Senior Editors, Ann R. Monjo and K.M. Rohan. Subscription rates, $15.00 for 4 issues; $25.00 for 8 issues; $30.00 for 12 issues. Single copy price $4.00. Discount 25% on 10 to 99 copies; 30% on 100 to 499; 35% on 500 to 999; 40% on 1,000 or more. Payment must accompany all orders. Add $1.75 for postage. USPS #238-340. Second-class postage paid at New York, N.Y. POST-MASTER: Send address changes to HEADLINE SERIES, Foreign Policy Association, 729 Seventh Ave., New York, N.Y. 10019. Copyright 1989 by Foreign Policy Association, Inc. Composed and printed at Science Press, Ephrata, Pennsylvania. Summer 1989.

Library of Congress Catalog No. 89-84292
ISBN 0-87124-127-7

Introduction

Assisting women has been a development concern for more than 15 years. Development is the process by which the material welfare of *all* people is improved over time. Among donor countries, the United States took the lead in drawing attention to the importance of women in development. The 1973 Percy amendment to the Foreign Assistance Act of 1961 called for the full integration of women into development projects and warned of the consequences if they were neglected. Following the International Women's Year conference in Mexico City in 1975 and the designation by the United Nations of a Decade for Women (1976–85), support for women increased. Projects for women and women's groups and organizations have multiplied throughout the Third World. Foundations in the United States and Europe have financed research on the social and economic conditions of women in developing countries.

The preparation of this issue of the HEADLINE SERIES was made possible by a grant from the Rockefeller Foundation. The production, translation into Spanish and distribution of the issue were made possible by a grant from Avon Products, Inc.

118252

3

Today gender issues are accepted as legitimate. Most donor agencies and nongovernmental organizations (NGOs) take women into account in their policies, and their institutional capacity to address women's needs has improved. Although developing-country governments as a whole have lagged behind international donors, many have made some efforts to improve women's status and living conditions. Women themselves have formed a broad-based international constituency increasingly able to lobby for their interests.

Despite these gains, the overall situation of women in developing countries has changed little. Most women continue to be poor and overworked. Their economic contributions are still overlooked, and they have reaped few of the benefits of economic growth. Donors, national governments and NGOs have yet to translate progress in acknowledging the importance of women in the development process into effective action. As the 1980s draw to a close, the implementation of gender-sensitive policies may be seriously hindered by economic crises and other global problems.

Prospects for the future of developing and developed countries have changed dramatically in this decade. Technological breakthroughs and East-West détente, on the positive side, and debt and recession, on the negative side, have affected the situation of the poor in general, and women in particular, in significant and often unpredictable ways. Understanding economic and political changes and how women have responded to them is essential to developing successful programs for alleviating their poverty. This understanding can be enhanced by a full appreciation of the history of development efforts for women and the evolution of earlier policies and projects.

In 1980 Elise Boulding wrote a HEADLINE SERIES entitled "Women: The Fifth World," in which she concluded that the failures of many economic projects in poor countries were attributable to neglect of women by governments and international agencies. Her conclusion remains valid. This book begins where Dr. Boulding left off, analyzing the economic contributions women make and their role in managing natural resources and promoting family health and welfare, and examining what international donors and national implementing agencies have and have not done, and why they have not accomplished more. It concludes with policy, institutional and project recommendations to increase women's access to the resources and opportunities that will move them and their families out of poverty.

The authors are grateful to Joyce L. Moock, associate vice-president of the Rockefeller Foundation, for her support. Thanks are due also to Sue Fleck, for her research, and Libby Lopez for her secretarial assistance. The book draws on publications from the International Center for Research on Women in Washington, D.C., in addition to those listed in the annotated bibliography. The authors, however, are solely responsible for its contents.

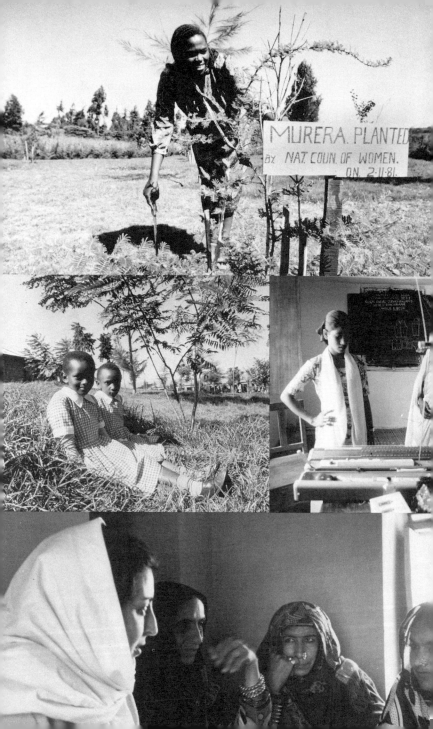

1

Women and Development

For women, who constitute more than 50 percent of the world's population, the years following World War II and the founding of the United Nations in 1945 opened new vistas of promise and equality. Conditions that had determined a woman's life for centuries began to change dramatically, particularly in developing countries. Former colonies in Africa, Asia, the Pacific and the Caribbean became independent countries. In many cases, these new nations adopted constitutions incorporating UN-inspired principles of equal rights for men *and* women. Other countries amended their constitutions to reflect the new commitment to equality and human rights. For three decades, growth and change were in the air.

The global economy expanded, profiting from an increase in trade, private and multilateral public investment and foreign aid flows from industrialized to developing countries. Greater integration of national economies and the extension of communications systems opened previously closed societies. Radio brought new ideas to remote rural areas and poor city neighborhoods. Increased modernization offered educational opportunities and health services to women and men. Education levels and life expectancy rose. For women with access to health care, new medical technologies freed them from frequent, often involuntary, pregnancies and fear of death in childbirth. Developments in microelectronics, communications technologies, the production of synthetic materials and the mechanization of labor-intensive processes altered the structure of the international economy with profound implications for both sexes.

In the late 1970s and early 1980s, the UN Decade for Women focused worldwide attention on women's needs and set standards for action. Although the decade yielded some reforms and resources, its major impact was on women themselves. Women's awareness of their condition and of the inequality between them and men has produced an extensive movement for change. This new movement differs from previous efforts in several respects. It has worldwide linkages, and its issues are broadly focused.

Beyond their rights as human beings, women are questioning the social structures and public policies that affect these rights. In particular, they are looking at issues of social justice, development and peace. Slowly, women are finding some support among men. Slowly, male-dominated development institutions are beginning to recognize the link between women's advancement and social and economic progress.

The Persistence of Poverty

Despite considerable economic and social progress, and advances in science and technology, poverty endures. According to the Overseas Development Council, a Washington-based policy research organization, nearly one billion men, women and children live in conditions of unmitigated poverty, fighting a daily battle against malnutrition, disease, illiteracy and high infant mortality rates. The poor of the 1980s are perhaps better endowed than the poor of past decades in that they are better organized and have more access to information, education and health services, but there are many more of them. Poverty, in general, and the poverty of women and children, in particular, continue to be major challenges facing the international community, national governments and women themselves.

Even though many women today are better educated, more

active economically and more successful professionally than they were a few decades ago, women continue to be seriously disadvantaged. In no major field of activity—economics, education, health or government—have women attained equal status with men. Social and economic structures in most countries still relegate women to second-class citizenship. Family codes, inheritance laws and labor legislation still discriminate against women, and repressive cultural traditions limit their participation in social and political life.

In many Third World countries, crushing poverty renders advances in health and education almost meaningless for women. Women, and the children for whom they are almost universally responsible, are poorer than men and have less access to resources and opportunities in both industrialized and developing countries. The economic plight of most women remains hidden in the home, but a rapidly rising minority have become the sole support for their families.

Roughly one third of all households in the Third World are headed by women, and in some regions, such as the cities of Latin America and the rural areas of some African countries, the percentage is closer to one half. Households headed by women, like those in the United States and Europe, are poorer than those headed by men. Families that depend on the husband's earnings have higher incomes because the wife contributes by working for pay or doing housework for free. Families headed by women must depend solely on a woman's lower earnings.

About three quarters of the poor—a majority of them women—inhabit rural areas. A large proportion are landless, unskilled, illiterate and unemployed or underemployed workers. The majority live in South Asia (Bangladesh, India, Nepal and Pakistan) and sub-Saharan Africa, with a small but growing number in Central America.

Misguided agricultural policies, including in some instances distorted prices benefiting urban consumers or an emphasis on export crops to the detriment of domestic food production, have increased the number of hungry people. Among the poorer countries whose economies are dependent on agriculture, those in

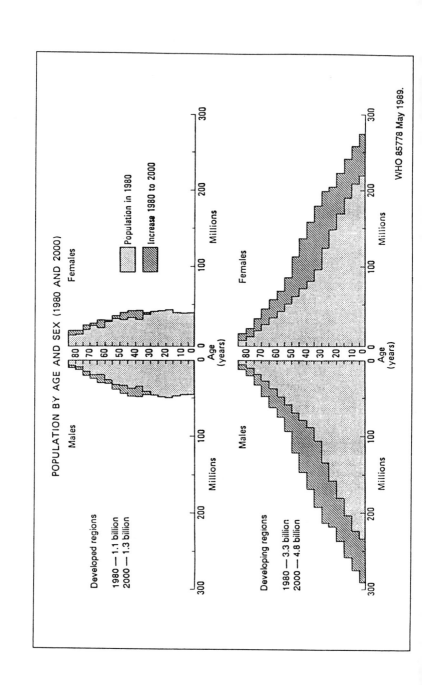

POPULATION BY AGE AND SEX (1980 AND 2000)

Africa in particular have suffered. From near self-sufficiency in food production in 1970, per capita agricultural production, including the cereals, roots and tubers that form the main staple of the diet, fell dramatically in the 1970s and early 1980s. Good weather produced above average harvests in 1988 and bumper crops are similarly expected in 1989. But better harvests are not helping the poor, particularly the women farmers who grow 60 to 80 percent of the food crops. They cannot afford to grow or buy enough food. Food consumption per person is in decline throughout most of Africa. In many countries there is a food shortage, and in some, large-scale famine.

The Population Link

Rapid population growth has outstripped economic growth and sorely strained the ability of governments to deliver vital services and generate employment. As numbers of births have multiplied, populations have become increasingly young. Because of better prenatal care for mothers and improved nutrition for infants, more children survive.

Improved public health measures—immunizations against childhood diseases and other illnesses, and partial control of endemic diseases such as malaria—have resulted in more people living longer. Partly due to health-related advances and partly to a continuing desire for large families in some countries, world population doubled from 2.5 billion in 1950 to 5 billion in 1987. More than 85 percent of that growth occurred in developing countries. Over 800 million jobs will have to be created by the turn of the century just to maintain current employment levels. For the world economy to grow, jobs above and beyond those available today will have to be created.

Population growth has created pressures on arable land and, combined with environmental degradation, has driven the rural poor in increasing numbers to cities in search of work and a better life. This migration has resulted in megacities such as Calcutta, Mexico City, Lagos and São Paulo, with populations ranging from 12 million to over 18 million people.

As populations and the demand for resources increase, the

quantity and quality of those resources—arable land and forests, lakes, rivers and streams, and animals—are being depleted and degraded. Water throughout the Third World is increasingly polluted by sewage and industrial wastes. In many countries, the so-called carrying capacity of the ecological system is sorely strained. The demands of too many people have exceeded the sustainable yields of forests, pastures and croplands, seriously threatening the life-sustaining resource base. Between 1950 and 1983, approximately 24 percent of Africa's forests disappeared. Each year in Latin America, 4 million hectares of forests are cleared or converted to other uses. Brazil alone accounts for 35 percent of the loss, but deforestation rates are rising in all countries, especially in Central America. In Asia over the past 30 years, Himalayan forests have declined by 40 percent. A shortage of fuelwood now affects 1.5 billion people in 63 countries. Those who suffer most as a result are women who must go farther and farther afield in their search for fuel.

Poverty in the Third World has been aggravated by wars and civil unrest. In Central America, Africa and the Middle East, conflicts have led to the death and displacement of millions of people, have destroyed ports, roads and other infrastructure, disrupted planting and harvesting, and damaged the environment. Most refugees are widowed or abandoned women with children who have been forced to flee their communities. Without means to support themselves, many eke out a bare living in refugee camps in their own or neighboring countries, with the help of international relief agencies. National governments, already strained to provide services and create employment for their own people, have been sorely taxed by the influx of refugees.

The Crisis of the 1980s

Unanticipated oil price hikes in 1973–74 and again in 1979 by the Organization of Petroleum Exporting Countries (OPEC) helped trigger a profound economic crisis in developing countries. Oil price increases set in motion a train of events that included heavy borrowing by developing countries from commercial banks, premised on expanding trade to repay loans. In developed

12

countries, attempts to control inflation arising from oil price increases led to a sharp contraction in international trade. This, in turn, resulted in a global recession that prevented many Third World countries from earning enough foreign exchange from exports to pay their debts. The outcome was a slowdown in foreign investment and a dramatic decline in overall economic growth rates that in many developing countries persists to this day. The crisis of the 1980s reversed the economic growth of developing countries, lasted far longer than anticipated, and compromised the position of industrialized economies as well.

While the crisis left the newly industrialized Asian countries— Taiwan, South Korea and Singapore—as well as Hong Kong, relatively untouched, it slowed the rate of economic growth considerably even in the better-off countries in Latin America and Africa. The disparity between the newly industrialized Asian countries and poorer economies in Africa and Latin America increased. Real per capita income in Latin America was lower in 1983 than in 1980. In Africa, real per capita access to resources was lower in 1979 than in 1970. Standards of living have deteriorated and poverty has increased. Both regions are deeply troubled by debt, recession, unemployment and underemployment. In some of the hardest hit Latin American cities, such as Lima, Peru, people cope by organizing communal kitchens; in others, people protest through mass demonstrations, strikes and urban violence.

Response of Western Governments and Donor Agencies

As the international economic crisis gathered momentum, the new Reagan Administration undertook major shifts in development assistance. These shifts were spurred in part by frustration that so many development projects appeared to have failed to alleviate poverty. The new Administration and many others in the international development community attributed the failures to flawed economic policies, excessive bureaucratization of Third World governments and project mismanagement. The Administration's antidotes were free-market policies and private- rather than public-sector programs. Setting the right market prices and

13

terms of trade, encouraging foreign investment, stabilizing currencies and implementing other macroeconomic changes were perceived as essential requirements for promoting economic growth. The U.S. focus and similar responses in European countries have dominated development strategy throughout the 1980s.

Disillusionment with past development efforts and the new interest in macroeconomic policy coincided with a radical decline in donor attention to alleviating poverty directly. The exceptions were child survival programs, which were expanded, and relief assistance for refugees of wars, famines and other natural disasters. When developing countries that had borrowed heavily from private and international banks during the 1970s could not pay their debts, aid agencies, in particular the World Bank and the International Monetary Fund (IMF), responded with long-term policies to stabilize recessionary economies and linked loans to structural adjustment programs. These policies called for increased domestic savings and improved public-sector efficiency and resource allocation; they also promoted economic incentives to reduce price distortions, such as increasing domestic farm prices to world levels and removing subsidies on items such as gasoline. These policies have had an impact on poor people that is just beginning to be understood.

To meet World Bank and IMF criteria, pay the interest on their debts and balance their budgets, Third World governments cut back drastically on productive investments, public and private-sector employment, and social services such as health, education and welfare programs. According to the United Nations Children's Fund (UNICEF), the world's least-developed countries have cut education budgets by 25 percent per head. The proportion of six-to-eleven-year-olds in school is falling. As wages decline and school fees increase, girls are at a particular disadvantage. Parents prefer to educate sons because their job prospects are better.

Cutbacks in employment and subsidies have moved middle-income families into poverty, and it is likely that they have had a severe impact on low-income groups, especially poor urban women and children who are the most vulnerable to changes in

Trends in Social Spending in Africa

Central government expenditure on education and health as a percentage of total government expenditure for selected African countries.

	Education		Health	
	1972	**1986**	**1972**	**1986**
Botswana	10.1	17.7	6.1	5.0
Burkina Faso	20.6	17.7	8.2	6.2
Ghana	20.1	23.9	6.3	8.3
Kenya	21.9	19.7	7.9	6.4
Lesotho	22.4	15.5	7.3	6.9
Malawi	15.8	11.0	5.5	6.9
Mauritius	13.5	13.4	10.3	7.7
Morocco	19.2	16.6	4.8	2.8
Tunisia	30.5	14.3	7.4	6.5
Uganda	15.3	15.0	5.3	2.4
Zaire	15.2	0.8	2.3	1.8

Source: World Bank, Africa News, May 1, 1989.

food prices and reductions in social programs. As governments remove food subsidies and lift price controls on basic commodities, food prices rise. Pregnant and nursing women, already at risk, probably have to decrease their food intake and the quality of their diet, with serious consequences for their own health and the health of their children. UNICEF reports that more than 1,000 children die each day in Africa. Less than half the population of the five Central American countries has access to basic health care, and one child in five dies before reaching age five.

On the other hand, many poor women (including those who head rural households) may have been relatively unaffected in the short term by cutbacks in welfare programs, their extreme poverty having prevented them from access to these programs in the first place. In the long term, however, their chances to move out of poverty are further reduced as the number of poor people increases.

The adjustment measures mandated by the World Bank and the IMF have had an impact on women's employment and income-earning opportunities. Women are often the last hired and first fired. They also find themselves "bumped down" the employment ladder when jobs of men on rungs above are eliminated. During times of prosperity, women fill jobs in the modern economy, but lose them to men during recessions. Women perform low-paid, menial work outside the modern economy—work not covered by modern labor regulations. Basically they take any work they can find to supplement a reduced household budget. Furthermore, when the economy declines, people cut back on expenditures. As a result of currency devaluation in Latin America, for example, many jobs in the service sector, in which women predominate, have been eliminated. Cutbacks in social service budgets also have more of an effect on women because they are more likely to be employed by agencies that deal with health, education and welfare.

Reductions in health services, coupled with the Reagan Administration's denial of funds to countries that permit abortion, have restricted women's access to safe contraception. The U.S. suspension of assistance to family planning programs such as those run by the International Planned Parenthood Federation (IPPF) and its affiliates and the UN Fund for Population Activities (UNFPA) in developing countries has been partially offset by increased support from European governments. Nevertheless, public health officials in many Third World countries claim that mortality rates of women due to complications arising from abortions are rising.

Assisting the Poor in the 1990s

The social costs of structural adjustment, now becoming apparent, have revived concerns of international aid-givers. The late 1980s find poverty once again high on the development-assistance agenda. The World Bank's 1987 annual report phrases this shift in priorities as one that seeks to integrate the poverty concerns of the 1970s into the growth and market-oriented concerns of the first half of the 1980s, emphasizing adjustment programs that protect the poor.

Progress in the 1990s depends in part on countries' reducing the burden of repaying their foreign debt so that they can invest their earnings to enable their economies to grow. Progress also depends on countries' abilities to meet more-tangible needs— adequate food, safe water, primary health care, basic education— and build the necessary human capital. Closer cooperation among governments, the private sector and development agencies, and decentralization of decisionmaking and resource allocation in developing countries are seen as critical to expanding services. With the dawn of a more cooperative era in superpower relationships, resources formerly allocated for military expenditures could be reallocated to development programs. These programs will need to confront the additional challenge of societies that have a growing percentage of old people and are using up nonrenewable resources.

Sustainable development, or development that does not damage the environment and meets the needs of the current generation without endangering future ones, has become a priority. Once thought to be a luxury developing countries could ill afford, environmental considerations are now critical. For this new strategy to be effective, international aid agencies will have to work directly with the poor, the men *and* women who form the basis of any sustainable development effort. Experience has shown that active participation on the part of beneficiaries is essential to the long-term success of development programs.

Sustainable development may be particularly suited to women precisely because of its emphasis on small-scale, diversified and ecologically sound production. The benefits would be especially marked in the case of poorer countries that have extensive agricultural bases (in sub-Saharan Africa and Central America) or fragile ecological zones (the semiarid countries south of the Sahara, Haiti, Nepal), and where women take care of household water, fuel and waste, and are the main producers of food for the family. Women's knowledge of water resources, seed varieties and tree uses can provide valuable information for the development of improved technologies. If they are to succeed, research on, and implementation of, sustainable ways to manage crops and natural resources will have to include women.

Urban growth and aging populations will place enormous pressure on the environment and increase demand for services and employment. In part because people are living longer and women are controlling their fertility more successfully, the over-55 population is growing in size and as a percentage of the total population. Today there are 370 million older persons in the developing world. In less than three decades, there will be more than one billion. The majority will be women residing in the cities of East Asia, the Caribbean and Latin America. Because of present high fertility rates, Africa will continue to have a young population for some time to come. Large cities will absorb most of the aging populations, and the "spillover" will remain in rural areas or will migrate. The number of megacities is expected to increase from less than a dozen today to fifty by the year 2000. Policies to expand water and sewage systems, sanitation and transportation services, health care for young and old, employment, and credit and technical assistance, including for self-help housing and the small-business sector, will be critical to prevent the establishment of a permanent urban underclass. Meeting these challenges will require the ingenuity of both public and private institutions.

Self-Help Organizations

Nongovernmental development organizations will continue to play a predominant role in coming decades by implementing projects that directly benefit the poor and by acting as an intermediary between them and their governments. Since the early 1970s, these organizations and grassroots groups have sprung up throughout the Third World. Their rapid increase in numbers in the 1980s can be attributed to both the gap left by the shift in donor concerns away from pro-poor strategies and the growing inability of developing-country governments to provide needed services. The multiplication of women's groups was a direct result of the UN Decade for Women. Assisted by private foundations, development agencies and governments, local NGOs have a growing capacity to carry out a wide range of programs and projects in small-business development, agriculture, self-help housing, primary health care and family planning services, and organizational and skills training. Local development organizations and grassroots groups, including those that are run by, and represent the interests of, women, are also increasingly effective in lobbying for or against policies that affect their interests.

Today there is general agreement that the economic contributions of women have been overlooked. There is also growing awareness that alleviating the poverty of women is linked to restoring economic growth. National governments and aid agencies are beginning to realize that women should be given equal access to resources and opportunities. Their focus on women's share of Third World poverty is long overdue. The importance of women's economic contributions has always been critical.

2

Women's Economic Contributions

Women are key to reducing hunger and poverty, promoting family welfare, finding sustainable solutions to the exploitation of natural resources and contributing to overall economic growth in the Third World.

Poor women seldom stop working. In a single day they may work in the fields, in a factory or market, and in their household and community. Poor women work longer hours than poor men. Because rural women have less access to time-saving technologies or services such as running water and electricity, they work even longer hours than urban women. The poorer the country, the more hours women work and the greater their contributions to family welfare and the economy. During times of economic crisis, it is women and children who increase their working hours to ensure family survival.

In parts of East Africa, women work up to 16 hours per day doing household chores, preparing food and growing 60–80 percent of the family's food, in addition to caring for children, the elderly, or the ill and disabled. In rural areas of the Philippines, women do similar work about 10 hours per day. Rural Javanese women work an estimated 11 hours per day compared to 8.5 hours for men. In Burkina Faso (formerly Upper Volta), in West

Africa, women have little more than one so-called free hour per day to take care of themselves, undertake community activities or socialize.

The table on page 23 summarizes information from studies on hours spent working by women in several countries in Africa, Asia and Latin America. The average number of hours ranges from 6 to 14 per day, with a median of 10.4 hours in rural Africa and 9.9 hours in rural Asia.

Men's daily schedules tend to vary much less than women's during their adult working life. Men work more or less a constant number of hours at farming or other work for cash income, and the remainder of their time is discretionary. Women must be more flexible. Their workday changes with the numbers and ages of children in the household and the annual cycle of agriculture and schooling.

As the table reveals, women divide their time between working outside the home—farming, in the market, at the office or factory —and at domestic chores as diverse as growing and processing food, hauling water and gathering firewood, taking children to the health clinic and preparing family meals.

As families grow in size and the need for cash income increases, much of the burden falls on women and older children. In the rural Philippines, for example, fathers spend only 1 or 2 hours daily in child care, food preparation, marketing and other chores, whether there is one child or seven in the family. Filipino women, however, spend about 2.5 hours per day working in the market-place, and 7–8 hours on domestic activities. When there are seven or more children, women work less at home and more in the market. They can do this because older children take over domestic chores. Men also reduce their child-care time (to about 10 minutes per day) but increase their discretionary or leisure time.

Behind Closed Doors

Benefits are often unequally distributed within families, with men and boys usually favored over women and girls. In times of scarcity, women and girls lose out in terms of quantity and quality of food as well as other resources. The reasons for this discrimina-

21

tion are grounded on the belief that males are more critical to family survival than females. It does not mean that men do not care for their womenfolk. But poverty dictates painful choices, and the belief that males are the breadwinners guides decisions in favor of men and boys. It is argued, for instance, that boys must attend school to prepare for the working world, and men must eat well to have the strength to earn family income.

Schooling for girls is not considered as important because they are not perceived as potential breadwinners. This myth goes hand in hand with the belief that women's education and women's work have little value and are of less importance to family welfare. But mothers', not fathers', education is the most important factor contributing to children's health. Moreover, whereas women prefer to spend their earnings on family needs, men tend to spend at least part of their income on entertainment and consumer goods such as radios and watches. These different spending preferences between women and men explain why, in many instances, the children of women who head poor households are healthier than the children in poor households headed by men.

Feeding the Hungry

Agriculture is the engine of growth for poor countries and poor people, and agricultural development is one of the most effective ways to alleviate hunger. Chronic food insecurity arising from rural poverty and a shortage of food supplies can be lessened by increasing the productivity of small farmers. Since women are often the principal growers of food, increasing domestic food production is synonymous with improving the productivity and income of women farmers.

It is estimated that women farmers grow at least 50 percent of the world's food and as much as 80 percent in some African countries. Between one third and one half of the agricultural laborers in the Third World are women. Roughly two thirds of women workers in developing countries are engaged in agriculture.

As a rule, women farmers work longer hours, have fewer assets and lower incomes than men farmers do, and have almost as many

Allocation of working hours of women in selected developing countries*

Country	Home and Subsistence Production[a]	Market and Agricultural Production[b]	Total
AFRICA			
Botswana	5.6	.6	6.2
Burkina Faso	5.7	4.1	9.8
Cameroon	5.7	3.9	9.6
Ivory Coast	5.1	6.9	12.0
Sudan	10.7	3.0	13.7
Tanzania	5.3	5.7	11.0
ASIA			
Bangladesh	6.7	5.0	11.7
India	4.0	2.0	6.0
Malaysia	10.0	1.8	11.8
Nepal	4.3	7.2	11.5
Philippines	7.4	.9	8.3
LATIN AMERICA			
Chile	5.4	7.0	12.4
Peru	n.a.	8.8	n.a.
Uruguay	5.2	6.9	12.1
Venezuela	n.a.	n.a.	9.3

*Based on studies completed in the 1980s.

a. Home and subsistence production is generally defined as food processing and cooking, housework, child care and health care for the family, as well as agricultural production that sustains the family.

b. Market and agricultural production is defined as activity designed to produce income for the household, such as handicrafts production, marketing, and either paid or unpaid labor in agricultural production directed toward market sales.

Sources: Luisella Goldschmidt-Clermont, *Economic Evaluations of Unpaid Household Work: Africa, Asia, Latin America and Oceania.* Geneva, International Labour Organisation, 1987.

Joanne Leslie, "Time Costs and Time Savings to Women of the Child Survival Revolution." Washington, D.C., International Center for Research on Women, July 1987.

dependents to support. The disparity is not due to lack of education or competence. Women farmers are poorer because their access to credit is limited. Without credit they cannot acquire productive assets, such as cattle, fertilizer or improved seeds, to increase the amount of arable land under cultivation and improve the productivity of their labor.

Policies that favor export crops have increased the participation of women in agriculture as both paid and unpaid laborers. Motivated to produce a surplus crop they can sell for cash, they are cultivating marginal lands. Rising food insecurity in Africa due to war and the migration of men has also increased women's participation: growing the food crops essential for survival in periods of economic stress is a task that falls heavily on the growing number of women farmers left behind.

Categories of Women Farmers

Women's roles in agriculture run the gamut from owner to wage laborer. Women who are *farm owners* and *managers* make decisions about production, devote a major portion of their time to farming, and are responsible for most agricultural tasks. Women farmers in Africa are most likely to fall into this category because of the absence of men, including husbands. In Western Kenya, for example, approximately 40 percent of the farms are managed by women. The remaining 60 percent are jointly managed by husband and wife. Farms with a man present in Kenya and throughout the Third World, for that matter, are far more likely to receive credit and agricultural extension services than farms managed by women. Even the most productive female farm managers receive few services. Thirty-three percent of women farm managers in Western Kenya have adopted a high-yield variety of maize but have never been visited by an extension agent. In contrast, only 3 percent of the male-managed farms that have adopted this variety have not been visited. When services are provided to male farmers only, women's productivity suffers by comparison.

A similar profile of female farm managers emerges in Botswana. Because men migrate to South Africa to work in the mines, 43

Labor-intensive work: A young Jamaican woman pulverizing cassava—which yields a nutritious starch—at the Bammy Bread Cooperative.

UN Photo/Milton Grant

percent of the farms are managed by women with children. These farms earn less than half the income of male-managed farms. Furthermore, the men own three times as many cattle as the women. Because women have fewer draft animals, they cultivate less land.

Women *farm partners* share responsibility for agricultural production with another household member, usually the husband. Decisions are made collaboratively. Both partners devote a major portion of their labor to farming, and tasks, though often divided by sex, are complementary. Studies undertaken in Nepal show that women farm partners make about 40 percent of the agricultural decisions and, in another 10 percent of the cases, the partners decide jointly. In Thailand, men and women share decisionmaking about marketing and credit for agricultural production. In some communities in Guatemala, women's traditional involvement in harvesting leads to joint decisionmaking regarding production.

Women *farm workers* are unpaid family laborers. Husbands or other relatives make the major decisions; they also take the profits. Women's tasks, though essential to production, are limited to chores that vary with the seasons. In periods of peak labor needs, women work on the family plot.

Women who work as *wage laborers* constitute a growing segment of the agricultural labor force. These women work for a daily wage or are paid according to output. In Sri Lanka, 72 percent of the women who work in agriculture are employed on tea plantations. They earn three quarters of the wages paid to men. Similarly, in India, 50 percent of the workers on tea plantations are women and are paid less than their male coworkers. Export fruit companies in Chile and Costa Rica rely almost exclusively on women for harvesting, processing and packing fruits. There, too, they are paid less.

Women make up 40 percent of the wage laborers in the tobacco industry in Honduras and almost 90 percent of the wage laborers in coffee. Farm owners in western Honduras claim they hire women because they are more responsible and reliable than men, better at picking coffee and tobacco, and work for less pay.

Agricultural Modernization

Agricultural modernization, such as the introduction of new technology, higher-yielding seeds, new cash crops or export commodities, can be both beneficial and harmful to women. When rice was introduced as a cash crop in Cameroon, it increased women's workload but it also raised their incomes. (However, the net increase was only 25 percent of the increase in men's incomes.) But in the Shaba region of the Zaire copper belt, the introduction of a high-yielding variety of maize proved disadvantageous to women. In Zaire, as in many other African countries, women and men traditionally farm different plots and have different responsibilities: women are in charge of the home gardens that provide a substantial portion of food for the family; men grow maize and other cash crops. The new variety of maize increased production and created the need for additional labor. Women furnished the labor, but because the maize was planted in the men's fields, men kept the profits. With the additional demands on their time, women had fewer hours to spend raising food crops for their families. Thus, the shift of women's labor to men's plots lowered the family's nutritional standards.

The introduction of vegetables for export in Guatemala is another illustration of the complex effects of agricultural modernization on women farmers. In Guatemala in the mid-1970s, an agribusiness firm provided seeds and credit to farmers in three communities to grow cauliflower, broccoli and snow peas for export, and it organized a cooperative to deliver seeds and fertilizer and purchase the crop. In Guatemala, men and women do not usually farm separate plots: wives provide unpaid labor for husbands and earn income for household expenses from other activities. In one of the communities, Chimachoy, women traditionally were market vendors, an activity that provided them with an independent source of income. With the introduction of the agribusiness project, many women gave up market vending. Instead, they spent two to three days a week planting, weeding and picking cauliflower. They were not invited to join the cooperative, and they were not paid for their labor.

In the neighboring village of Santiago, women customarily grew vegetables to sell locally. When the cooperative was organized, they became members, receiving cash payment for their crops from the agribusiness firm. By 1985, however, the cooperative had grown so big that the firm changed its methods from paying in cash to weekly payments by check. The majority of the women farmers were illiterate and could not open checking accounts. Therefore, their husbands were given their checks, which they did not necessarily share.

The experience of the Santiago cooperative illustrates how new technologies can have unexpected consequences and are not always gender neutral. In this case, a single procedure—payment by check, which was simply seen as a way to manage a growing business more efficiently—resulted in women workers losing their pay to men.

Placing a Value on 'Invisible' Work

The economic contributions of women's invisible work, significant as they are, are often unheralded. Agricultural censuses in most Third World countries grossly undercount women who provide seasonal wage labor on farms and plantations. In Honduras, for example, where observation at harvesttime revealed that women did most of the work, a 1970 agricultural census indicated the majority of paid workers were men. Farm owners confirmed the failure of the census to count women workers. In the Honduran department of Copán, the census recorded only 642 female workers. Field estimates based on interviews with owners, however, came to around 11,000 women workers. The 1970 census failed to record accurately the number of women workers for two reasons. First, individuals were classified as economically active in terms of their principal occupation, and the majority of women reported their principal occupation as housewife. Second, the census was carried out in a period of slack agricultural activity in order to find people at home. Because women often work seasonally and in periods of intense rather than slack activity, they were not employed on farms at the time of the census. Women's invisible wage labor in Copán was essential to grow and harvest 24 percent of Honduras's yearly tobacco production and roughly 6,000 tons of coffee. By working for lower wages than men, women wage laborers subsidized this production.

Growing awareness of the importance of unpaid labor by women in developing countries has resulted in independent studies that attempt to quantify women's economic contributions. These studies consider subsistence activities (e.g., growing food for family consumption) and domestic ones (such as housework) that can be delegated to a paid outsider. They measure the activity either by the number of hours women spend at work, the economic value of this time (what wage a person would earn if hired to do the work), the volume of their production (the amount of firewood collected), or the value of what a woman produces (the price of the cassava that women process).

Using the value of time as a measure, it has been estimated that in urban Pakistan women's domestic activities contribute approximately 35 percent of the gross national product (GNP) and 38 percent of household cash income. Women's subsistence activities, without considering domestic ones, amount in some rural areas of Botswana, Cameroon and Nepal to 54–70 percent of total household income; domestic activities contribute another 30 percent. In rural Malaysia, subsistence activities, including domestic ones, contribute 56 percent of household monetary income. In the Pakistani city of Lahore, women's domestic activities amount to 38 percent of household monetary income and 36 percent of the GNP.

Women's economic contributions count most in poor families. Women in poor families contribute proportionately more to household income through domestic and paid work than do wealthier women. In the Peruvian sierra, for example, women from families with little land provide 35 percent of family labor in agriculture, whereas women from middle income or rich farm families provide only 21 percent.

Managing Scarce Resources

Because rural women depend on natural resources, including water, fuel, pastures and home gardens, for their livelihood, they contribute to their management and are especially affected by the deterioration of the physical environment. In urban areas as well, women use water and other resources more than men. For all practical purposes, however, the world environmental movement has yet to acknowledge women's role in conservation. As an illustration, the 1987 report of the World Commission on Environment and Development, chaired by Norwegian Prime Minister Gro Harlem Brundtland, which set the world agenda for sustainable and environmentally sound growth, does not mention women's responsibilities and contributions.

In many societies, it is women who carry out and pass on ecologically sound methods of agriculture that are based on their extensive knowledge of traditional seed varieties, tubers, trees and crop systems. They often grow medicinal plants and store emergency supplies of food and water for times of shortage. Because women are accustomed to changing their workday patterns to accommodate new demands, they are more able to cope with food shortages than men.

Women and Food Security in Africa: The Case of Cassava

Women do 70 to 80 percent of the planting, weeding and harvesting and 100 percent of the processing of cassava, a root crop critical in times of food scarcity. Compared to wheat and rice, crops that men control, limited monies have been devoted to research on cassava and for extension services. Cassava is easy to plant and weed, but demands time to harvest. Processing is very labor intensive. The natural cyanide in the tuber must be washed out, and approximately 18 five-hour days are required to process 1 ton of cassava into *gari,* a paste that can be eaten. Research has concentrated on producing bigger tubers or high-yielding varieties, ignoring the development of processing technologies that would increase both the productivity of women farmers and the demand for, and price of, the crop. Cassava illustrates four issues critical to understanding women's role in agriculture.

1. The extent of women's participation in food production and their contributions to food security.

2. The heavy demands farming places on women's time and labor.

3. The willingness of women to grow crops which have little or no economic payoff but enable poor families to eat during periods of food scarcity.

4. The general tendency to assign fewer resources to crops grown by women.

Women in Islamic northern Nigeria, for example, have a range of responses to food crises. Generations of experience have provided them with knowledge of cropping practices suited to different weather patterns and emergency conditions. When food is scarce, they change the cropping pattern, find off-farm opportunities and cooperate with other women to feed their families. Soil degradation in Nigeria, as well as in other parts of Africa, has caused women to shift from maize to cassava production. The species of cassava produced has less nutritional value than maize, but women use more parts of the plant in meal preparation so that the tuber provides increased calories and proteins.

Women also transplant and nurture trees—in part because they are in charge of home gardens where trees are often grown and in part because the task of tree planting and nurturing has few economic returns. Because women are used to working without immediate payment in cash or in kind, they cope better with the delayed nature of returns on investment implicit in tree planting and protection.

More than a decade ago, a hurricane devastated the north coast of Honduras, washing out forests and soils near the city of San Pedro Sula. The men migrated to the city in search of work; the women stayed behind and took charge of reforestation, to the surprise of the development agencies. Organized in housewives' clubs by Caritas, the social action agency of the Catholic Church, women built terraces and planted a variety of fruit trees to contain soil erosion and restore the natural resource base. Honduran women were willing to invest time and accept delayed economic returns.

In Asia and Africa, women are leading efforts to reverse the destruction of forests. Kenya's Greenbelt Movement has established 50 nurseries, producing 2,000 to 10,000 seedlings per year and 239 "green belts" throughout the country. Women's organizations are actively involved in the Kenya energy NGO, whose objectives are to safeguard energy supplies and promote reforestation. In the state of Uttar Pradesh, in northern India, women are increasingly active in the Chipko Andolan movement to plant trees to be used for fuel and fodder.

Another reason for women's concern with deforestation, studies have shown, is that they are particularly affected by its consequences. In Africa, for example, where the number of trees felled outpaces new trees planted by a ratio of 29 to 1, women must spend more time and travel farther to gather firewood as trees become scarcer. They often have to walk up to 10 kilometers and spend 5–8 hours every 4–7 days collecting wood for fuel. This task, along with fetching water, can consume 400–500 calories per day, substantially decreasing the time and energy women have to do other work.

The additional drain on their time affects women's as well as children's welfare. In less than a decade, the loss of trees in Nepal has meant that women must spend an extra hour per day to collect firewood. By cutting into the time women have available for cooking and food preparation, deforestation has contributed to increased child malnutrition.

Promoting Family Health

Many of the tasks that women perform as homemakers and mothers are critical for the prevention and treatment of childhood diseases and malnutrition. In developing countries at least 75 percent of all health care takes place within the family. It is women, particularly in their role as mothers, who carry the responsibility for family health. Since health services in rural areas are limited, the poor generally do not have access to hospitals and modern medicine. Women treat common diseases and injuries, and take children and the sick to a health center if there is one.

Generally aware of women's vital role in health care, health ministries in many developing countries rely on women to transmit new technologies to their families and communities. What planners of programs to train women as health workers often ignore is that women, in addition to providing health care, must also earn income to purchase food and medicines. Although women usually are not paid to perform community health work, managers of primary health care programs frequently ask them to spend substantial amounts of time learning how to do so. They fail to realize that women may confront serious time conflicts when they are also asked to attend health lectures. Many women who do attend training hope it will lead to paid employment as government health workers.

International health and nutrition experts often claim women's work outside the home has a negative impact on children's health. They argue that breastfeeding, essential to ensuring the health of infants in poor families, is incompatible with women's income-generating activities. Recent studies question this claim. These studies show that both women who work for pay outside and those who stay at home have similar customs. Cultural traditions and preferences, rather than whether a woman works for pay, guide decisions about breastfeeding and weaning of children.

More importantly, these studies show that poor women who work for decent and regular wages purchase high quality foods and have healthier children than women who do not. Furthermore, increases in income of the poorest women translate into improved child health much more often than comparable increases in male incomes.

Weathering Economic Crises

In periods of economic recession, poor women work harder and join the work force in greater numbers to compensate for real losses in family income. This contribution is not limited to poor women in the Third World. Women joined the labor force in great numbers to help their families endure the Great Depression of the 1930s in the United States and to help them weather the oil-related recessions of the 1970s in Europe.

Since the beginning of the Latin American debt crisis in 1982, the increase in women's participation in Latin American labor markets has been more rapid than men's. And in urban areas throughout the Third World, large numbers of women have joined the "informal sector." Informal-sector workers include market vendors, food peddlers and artisans—the lowest paid, lowest-level occupations. In general, they are the self-employed who operate on street corners or run a restaurant or shop out of their homes. Informal-sector occupations, in contrast to regular jobs in a factory or office, do not offer social security or employment benefits; they are not covered by permits or licenses, employment contracts or guarantees. People who work in the informal sector usually do not abide by or have to contravene municipal regulations (such as business permits) to operate. They also rarely have access to credit, skills training or technical assistance that could make their work more productive and re-

---

Coping with Economic Crises: Peru and Chile

Women living in slums surrounding Lima and Santiago have organized communal kitchens. Groups of 15–50 members buy and prepare food collectively. Families pay according to the number of meals requested. Communal kitchens save costs and relieve women of shopping for food and preparing and serving meals, thus freeing time for income-earning employment. Some communal kitchens have nutrition-education programs and growth-monitoring systems for children. Others offer literacy programs and sewing workshops. *The New York Times* recently reported that in Lima alone there are 1,500 kitchens in the city's 24 districts.

munerative. Women who work in this sector have even more limited access than men to resources.

Because informal-sector activities are seldom recorded, it is difficult to know exactly how many people are involved. Recent estimates claim that more than half the jobs in large Latin American cities fall into this category. Studies further suggest that between 1981 and 1983 the informal sector grew by about 20 percent, but the average income of persons employed in this sector fell by about 21 percent. Studies also estimate that women's participation in the informal sector in La Paz, Bolivia, grew from 37 percent in 1976 to 48 percent in 1983, and that between 51 percent and 62 percent of workers in informal-sector occupations in Mexico are women. In Ecuador and Honduras, women make up about 40 percent of the workers.

Women's contributions are all the more impressive because they have received so little assistance from governments or international donor agencies. The limited assistance women have received dates from two events in the early 1970s—the beginnings of an international focus on poverty and the designation by the UN of a Decade for Women, starting with an International Women's Year in 1975.

3

Development Assistance— Past and Future

In the early 1970s development planners began to challenge the assumptions of the 1960s that the transfer of capital and technologies from developed countries to developing countries would help raise the latter's living standards. Even though developing countries had slightly exceeded the growth targets the international donor community had set for the 1960s, there were widening disparities among countries. Because Third World countries lacked such basic infrastructure as roads, schools, factories, a trained work force and public utilities, the successes of the Marshall Plan for Europe's reconstruction after World War II could not be repeated.

Robert S. McNamara, then president of the World Bank, took the lead in calling for an attack on Third World poverty. In his address to the World Bank board of governors in 1973, he focused on the urgent need to reduce unemployment and underemployment, improve income distribution, develop appropriate or simpler, less-expensive technologies that the poor could use and afford, promote rural development and address people's basic needs.

The World Bank began to invest in education, health and family planning, and allocated substantial resources to rural infrastructure, such as roads and electricity, and small-farmer agriculture to increase productivity. It initiated rural development projects that integrated inputs and services for the poor, including fertilizer and credit, roads and schools, skills training and nutrition, and took the lead in research on basic human needs. Other bilateral and multilateral donors followed suit. Because of the focus on poverty alleviation, funds became available to increase the productivity and incomes of the poor. International relief agencies and private voluntary organizations began to develop their own small-scale economic projects.

A Decade for Women

Despite the fact that poor women were performing much of the labor, donor agencies in the 1970s focused almost exclusively on men. They continued to see women as dependents with children or as pregnant or nursing mothers—as consumers of services rather than producers of goods. It took the UN Decade for Women to begin to make the economic role of women visible to Third World governments and the development community. The Decade for Women, together with books such as Ester Boserup's *Woman's Role in Economic Development* and new antipoverty strategies, focused long-overdue attention on women's poverty and their economic contributions.

The idea for an international women's year grew out of a proposal made by a group of women's organizations at a 1972 meeting of the UN Commission on the Status of Women in Geneva, Switzerland. Subsequently, the UN General Assembly voted to make 1975 the International Women's Year, and then, after a conference held in Mexico City, to make 1976–85 the UN Decade for Women, with three goals: equality, development and peace.

The 1975 International Women's Year conference and the IWY Tribune of NGOs that met concurrently in Mexico City were attended by 6,000 women and men from 133 nations. The meetings raised the consciousness of women and their expectations for the future. Participants approved a World Plan of Action that called for an increase in literacy, especially in rural areas; equal access to education at all levels, including vocational training in agriculture and industry; increased employment opportunities and a reduction in discrimination in terms and conditions of employment; equal opportunity to vote, seek elected office and serve in policymaking positions; and increased social services. Governments were urged to establish appropriate offices to accelerate the process.

Larger conferences and parallel NGO meetings were held at mid-decade in 1980 in Copenhagen, Denmark, and in 1985 in Nairobi, Kenya, to assess progress and ensure continuing attention to women's status and needs. At the 1985 conferences in Nairobi, which drew 16,000 women from 150 countries, government delegates drafted a document, "Forward-Looking Strategies for the Advancement of Women," that, despite conflicting ideologies, was accepted by the United States and other participating governments. The "Strategies" seek equal partnership between men and women by the year 2000 and call again for achieving the objectives set forth in the World Plan of Action.

Women Working Together

The Decade for Women raised women's consciousness and spurred them to action. Throughout the world, women joined together in formal organizations and informal grassroots groups to undertake a wide range of political and economic actions on their own behalf. In the process they gained self-confidence, new skills, the ability to carry out economic projects and the capacity to organize and pressure for change. Women have pressured governments to hire and promote women professionals, include women's needs in development programming and establish special offices or bureaus to integrate women's issues into policy planning. But because they lack funds, staff and political clout, these government offices and bureaus remain largely ineffective.

Today, the world of women's organizations includes arms of political parties that lobby for the integration of women's political, economic and legal interests; worker- and peasant-based movements or federations, most of which have a political agenda, such as guaranteeing the minimum wage for women or their access to land through reform programs; institutions that carry out research on women's issues; and women's studies associations that have rescued women's history from oblivion. The work of the latter two, by revealing the true circumstances of women's lives, has had some impact on governments and donor agencies and a major impact on women activists and development practitioners. Due in large part to the work of women researchers, women's work in agriculture and commerce is now well documented, as are their contributions to family income. Research on women who head households in Third World societies has influenced aid donors to finance income-generating projects and has been used by women activists throughout the world to justify attention to poor women and their economic plight. Women's movements have also mobilized around single issues: peace, nuclear energy, sexual exploitation, sex tourism and racism. Finally, poverty- and equity-oriented women's development organizations have emerged as a direct result of donor support. These organizations provide a wide range of services to poor women in rural and urban areas. In spite of the diversity of cultures in which they live and the different contexts in which they operate, women increasingly have come to recognize and share a common belief that equality, development and peace are not possible without their direct participation.

Donors Helping Women

Following the Mexico City conference in 1975, multilateral and governmental agencies as well as private foundations began to address women's economic needs by providing some short-term project support to poor women. In the late 1970s and early 1980s these agencies showed a marked preference for working through nongovernmental organizations, particularly women's groups, in the developing countries rather than through governments. Donors had a variety of objectives. The World Bank emphasized income-generating projects as a means to reduce fertility and contain population growth. The International Labor Organiza-

> ### Coping with Economic Needs: Honduras
>
> Since the late 1970s the Federation of Honduran Peasant Women (FEHMUC) has run community health programs in four departments of the country. Initially, FEHMUC hired nurses to train rural women to provide primary care, including nutrition education, maternal/child health, first aid and basic sanitation, to their communities. The health workers earned income and restocked their kits by charging for medicines. They made bulk purchases of pharmaceuticals in the capital city of Tegucigalpa. In 1984, with inflation on the rise, the women found it too expensive to restock their kits. There was also a nationwide shortage of medicines, so they turned to natural medicines and traditional remedies. Small grants from donors enabled several to receive training from the "barefoot doctors" program at the University of Zacatecas in Mexico, and Mexican specialists in homeopathy, acupuncture and other traditional techniques came to Honduras to train FEHMUC health workers.

tion (ILO) was concerned with the equality of men and women in the workplace and workers' recognition of their family responsibilities. These concerns guided ILO research into technologies to relieve the drudgery of rural women's domestic work. The U.S. Agency for International Development's (AID) interest in increasing women's economic participation in order to encourage overall economic growth prompted it to give preference to small-scale enterprise projects. AID has worked with both governments and nongovernmental organizations, but its commitment to the latter has increased over time.

Private foundations channeled most of their assistance to women's organizations and to male-run organizations which had women's projects. The United Nations Development Fund for Women (UNIFEM), established after the Mexico City conference, also increased its work with nongovernmental development agencies between 1978 and 1984.

Projects Designed for Women

Three types of projects were prevalent during this period: small and microenterprise projects, which provided credit and technical assistance mostly to women vendors and artisans; income-generating projects, primarily offering skills training and other services to groups of women; and vocational education or training of various kinds.

Small and microenterprise projects for women vendors and artisans have been the most successful in expanding economic opportunities for women. Worldwide, they have reached a relatively large number of beneficiaries and provided the necessary resources to increase women's business income. The Working Women's Forum (WWF) in Madras, India, is an organization that has been successful in this field. The forum was founded in 1977 to improve the entrepreneurial skills of poor working women. WWF provides training, material inputs, credit and extension services. (It also organizes social services such as child care, education, health and family planning.) Acting as guarantor to local banks, the forum has enabled over 10,000 women to receive short-term loans for more than 65 small-scale businesses and trades. An evaluation of the WWF program showed that earnings have increased 50 percent in existing enterprises, 2,800 new jobs or businesses have been created, and the loan-repayment rate is 95 percent.

The objective of income-generating projects is to bring women who are outside the cash economy into market production. Groups of poor women receive training in organization and in traditional female skills such as sewing, crafts or food processing; in addition they receive credit for collective production and marketing. The Federation of Voluntary Agencies in San José, Costa Rica, established in 1969 to train volunteers for its member agencies, sponsored organizational training for poor women in urban neighborhoods of the city. With donor funds, and at the request of women participants, 11 small sewing groups, ranging in size from 5 to 25 members, were organized. Some groups were trained to produce school or 4-H club uniforms, pants or children's shirts under contract to local factories. Others sold their products on the open market or to stores. Because the factory contracts were exploitative, some groups were not able to earn enough to pay for light and water in their workplaces, nor did they have access to standard labor benefits. Other groups suffered from a lack of working capital and markets. Most of the women

were unable to produce quality goods and had administrative
problems. Only one group was successful in increasing its
members' incomes.

In another case, a national affiliate of an international NGO
organized 50 rural women into a cooperative in Western Kenya to
produce banana-fiber rings for sale as potholders in Nairobi.
Because the unit cost of the fiber was 3 shillings and the retail
price of the potholders was 2.50 shillings, the women lost a half
shilling on every potholder sold. This did not include the cost of
their labor—which the women volunteered.

The two projects failed for similar reasons. The development
agencies did not have technical expertise or the financial resources
to hire expertise. Furthermore, their objective was to enable
women to earn *extra* income for the household rather than
establish successful business enterprises. These projects survived
because they achieved, at least in the short term, the social
objective of organizing and training women in group skills. On
the whole, income-generating projects have been ineffective for
poor women.

Vocational Education

The record of vocational education projects is also mixed.
Many projects fail because trainers do not have the necessary
technical capability and because there is no demand for the skilled

labor they are developing. Other job training projects fail because trainees lack capital to set themselves up in business afterward.

A vocational training program in the Dominican Republic, for example, was run by a nongovernmental organization which had no technical qualifications to provide job training. The program offered sewing and crafts. One month after completing the course, 89 percent of the women were still unemployed because there was no demand for their skills in the labor market. A similar program in Brazil was also unsuccessful due to the failure to link job training to job placement.

These and other projects traditionally designed for women have done little to change the occupational and wage structure or the sexual division of labor. They have not expanded women's economic options, nor have they helped women enter higher-priced product markets or the formal sector of the economy. The projects have, however, provided organizational, management and leadership training, resources that would not otherwise have been available to poor women, and in some cases, training in marketable skills.

Most efforts on the part of aid agencies to expand women's economic opportunities have concentrated on increasing the productivity of women workers rather than the demand for women's labor, and have taken the form of pilot projects rather than national or regional programs. Many donors have not worked with government agencies in developing countries because most are unreceptive to women's problems. These agencies, however, are key to generating formal-sector employment, formulating labor-intensive policies, and implementing national programs. The nongovernmental focus, nevertheless, has been a rational choice for donors because it is easier for them to influence and work with NGOs than with government agencies.

Women Helping Women

Women's service organizations, an outcome of the relief movement initiated after World War II, have existed for years in most countries. Generally, they have been organized to address welfare issues. For example, Maendeleo Ya Wanawake (MyW), the largest women's voluntary association in Kenya, was set up before independence by a small group of European women settlers to promote the advancement of African women and raise African living standards. MyW soon became an African organization, but the welfare legacy remained. MyW, which coordinates women's clubs around the country, is still primarily staffed by volunteers who perform charitable activities.

Another example of a women's service organization is the All India Women's Conference (AIWC). Established in 1926, AIWC currently has more than 100,000 members. Its objective is to contribute to the "general welfare of women and children in India" and its activities include organizing conferences and educational programs and providing welfare services.

With the onset of the Decade for Women and the availability of funds for antipoverty projects, both MyW and AIWC and their sister organizations in other countries began to implement small-scale income-generating projects for poor women. They have experienced the same problems as the Federation of Voluntary Agencies in Costa Rica, and for the same reasons. Their income-generating projects have survived because they meet the welfare objectives these relief-oriented organizations are equipped to implement.

Traditional service organizations, nonetheless, have provided important educational, health, nutrition and maternal/child care services to women. Such organizations usually have access to resources and policymakers, are well organized and have large memberships and systematic methods for transferring organizational skills and building leadership. They can (although they do not always do so) function as pressure groups, lobbying for the rights and needs of women, and can act as a link between poor women and policymakers at the national level. For example, as a result of effective pressure by MyW, the Kenyan government granted land rights to women in 1979.

The poverty- and equity-oriented women's development organizations that emerged from the Decade for Women are different in that they seek the full integration of women into the political and economic life of their countries. Indeed, their goal is the economic emancipation of women. They recognize that access to resources is essential for economic autonomy and that economic autonomy can lead to autonomy in other areas of women's lives. Their collective experiences tend to confirm that separate funds and projects for women are a necessary first step to integration. Thus, they offer credit and technical assistance, legal aid, reproductive health care, and organizational, management and leadership training. Their economic projects compare favorably with many managed by male-run NGOs for poor men.

Two examples of successful women's development organizations are the Association for the Development and Integration of Women (ADIM), founded in Lima, Peru, in 1979, and Women's World Banking (WWB), founded in 1980 by a group of delegates from nine countries who attended the Mexico City conference. The objective of ADIM is to promote women's self-esteem and economic self-sufficiency. Supported by AID and others, ADIM provides credit to street and market vendors and women with small businesses such as bakeries and grocery shops in their homes. To date ADIM has made over 10,000 loans, averaging U.S. $150, to nearly 3,000 beneficiaries. The value of these loans tops $1.5 million, and 1,325 jobs have been created. Like the Working Women's Forum in Madras, the loan repayment rate is over 90 percent. ADIM also offers legal aid to battered wives and women abandoned by their partners, and runs a clinic that provides quality reproductive health care.

WWB is a global support network for women who want to start small businesses but lack the capital, management skills and self-confidence to do so. WWB and its 92 affiliates on six continents provide technical assistance, training and credit guarantees to local banks which assume 25 percent of the risk in making loans to women entrepreneurs. In Colombia, the five-year-old WWB operation has made 19,000 loans, 68 percent of them to women, with an overall default rate of less than 15 percent.

Strengths and Weaknesses of Women's Organizations

Women's organizations tend to share the following strengths: they are effective in reaching poor women; they encourage

In Santo Domingo, Dominican Republic, a store displays the handiwork of women being helped by a UN Voluntary Fund project—one of several hundred initiated in Asia, the Pacific, Latin America and the Caribbean.

women's participation in decisionmaking at staff and beneficiary levels; they provide a supportive environment that encourages the learning of nontraditional skills, both technical and managerial. They allow poor women to "catch up" without male competition and graduate into the formal economy by providing access to modern services or productive resources. A salient example of the latter is credit, which allows women to compete for funds with women with similar borrowing qualifications.

Perhaps the most important achievement of women's organizations is their ability to mobilize women and raise awareness of gender issues and build self-confidence, thus enabling them to take greater economic and political responsibility. In societies where women are accustomed to thinking of themselves as second-class citizens, these are considerable accomplishments.

Women's organizations also tend to share generic weaknesses: limited financial resources, limited organizational and technical expertise, and limited access to the networks that allocate resources and knowhow. Because these organizations are generally on the fringes of development and financial establishment networks, they lack institutional clout. This is reflected in the small size of their projects and their difficulty in raising funds, particularly in their own countries. For these reasons, women's organizations, with their well intentioned but inadequately funded and poorly staffed projects, run the risk of further isolating or marginalizing poor women. In a sense, women's organizations share similar barriers with the poor women they help—limited access to resources.

Unfinished Business

Although the Decade for Women focused attention on women's poverty, international donors and Third World governments have done little to alleviate it. They have not addressed the policy and institutional changes nor committed the funds needed to bring about equality and increase women's access to opportunities and resources. In particular, donors have not assisted women farmers. Funds have not been allocated for research on food crops women grow and process or for extension services, which seldom reach women. The necessary legal reforms that would enable women to gain title to land or access to credit have not been enacted, although some countries have passed legislation revising family codes or labor legislation for the benefit of women.

With few exceptions, international development agencies continue to view women's economic roles in terms of earning "pin money" for the household. Although some donors have provided credit and technical assistance to women vendors, or for agroprocessing or crafts, most have supported projects that focused on women in their domestic role or tried to generate income from traditional female occupations, such as sewing. Almost universally, these projects have failed to produce sustained income. In part, this is because until recently the institutional capacity to address women's economic roles has been limited; in part, it is because the task is a difficult one. It is much easier to implement social welfare projects than increase the productivity and incomes

46

of the poor because to do so means fighting vested interests and redistributing economic resources. Men may fear that increasing women's incomes will diminish the power they hold in the workplace and the family. There are also financial reasons why donor agencies and national governments have failed to address women's needs. It is mostly male donors who allocate resources, and by restricting their support to projects dealing with women's roles as mothers and nurturers or projects that view income generation as a secondary or "add on" activity, funders avoid having women compete with men for resources in productive sectors.

The Road Ahead

National governments, donor agencies and NGOs are beginning to understand that women are a poverty group with special needs and that the benefits of economic growth are not necessarily shared within the household. Today many donor agencies and NGOs admit that development programs generally have not benefited women and, in the process of delivering new technologies to men, have often deprived women of resources and income they previously controlled. Thus, the willingness of some agencies to tackle the gender implications of development is an important gain. In addition, the number of institutions and agencies able to address women's issues has increased.

Whether women should be integrated into existing programs or into women-only programs is debatable, but the issue has significant implications for the policies of governments and donor agencies. On the one hand, an AID evaluation of 102 projects over 10 years noted that women-only projects are best suited to deliver training but are less successful in increasing production and generating income. The evaluation argued for the integration of women into regular development programs, and concluded that projects that include women in proportion to their roles and responsibilities are more likely to achieve their goals than those that do not.

A 10-year evaluation of UNIFEM projects, on the other hand, concluded that the choice between *women-only* and *integrated* projects should be determined by women's cultural background and their level of training. UNIFEM further warned that when the choice is *for* integrated projects, agencies need to make sure that it is the *women* and *not* the funds that are integrated. In one Latin American country, for example, a new women's organization trying to establish a service center for rural women migrants in the capital city fell apart after the male director of the NGO refused to release funds to the women staff members. In another, an NGO received a grant to organize an association of market women's credit unions. Not only was the association never formed, but a high percentage of grant funds was diverted to unrelated activities.

Some international aid agencies are now moving beyond small women-only projects and experimenting with ways to institutionalize fully women's needs and incorporate women into their regular programs. AID, for example, has a mandate to address gender roles in its planning documents and is beginning to train program officers to integrate women into agricultural, income-generating and microenterprise programs. The Canadian International Development Agency (CIDA) and the United Nations Development Program (UNDP) have designated women a priority for the 1990s. The newly established Arias Foundation for Peace and Human Progress, in Costa Rica, will address the problems of women-headed households, in addition to its other activities. The Inter-American Development Bank has recently appointed a women-in-development officer. There are also the beginnings of a long-overdue focus by the World Bank on women's role in agriculture and a renewed interest in women's health. The medical and public health communities increasingly recognize that women are key to the health of families and must be involved in the promotion and dissemination of new technologies. As the 1980s draw to a close, there are encouraging signs.

4

Alleviating Women's Poverty:
An Agenda for the 1990s

Providing women with access to decently paid employment and productive resources (capital, land and technologies) is the most effective way to alleviate their poverty. Because of crucial links between women's work, family welfare and sustainable growth, these efforts will pay off handsomely. Increasing the demand for and the price of women's work and women's access to assets and modern-sector training, jobs and credit will require legal, policy and institutional reforms to eliminate discrimination against women. Donors must take into account the impact of laws and government policies on women's work and poverty, and the nature of sex discrimination in labor, product and financial markets. The project approach favored to date is clearly inadequate; projects alone cannot alleviate women's poverty.

The damage that structural adjustment programs may be inflicting on poor-women's work and incomes will also have to be mitigated by gender-sensitive policies and projects. Although women are critical to increasing the production and marketing of both domestic and exportable goods, structural adjustment programs tend to overlook their role. Efforts by donors and governments to cushion the negative effects of adjustment on vulnerable populations have yet to address the income-earning needs of poor women. They may be causing further impoverishment of women, and, therefore, reversing the very gains they intended to achieve.

Because there are critical differences in the types of work men and women do and in the way they use income, programs or projects aimed at the household or family are not as effective in alleviating women's poverty, nor in most cases the poverty of children, as programs that focus on women. When they raise women's productivity and income, they tend to produce benefits for the entire family.

Agriculture

Access to technical assistance, credit for purchasing improved seeds and fertilizer, and draft animals can raise women farmers' productivity. Simple technologies, such as wells for water and small mills that grind grain, which decrease women's workloads, can also help raise the standard of living and welfare of their households, increase the demand for goods and services (as well as the demand for labor) in rural areas and improve distribution of income. Increasing productivity also requires policy and program changes, in addition to research and extension services.

Enlightened *agricultural policies* that will benefit women include price incentives for crops traditionally grown by women; price and other policy incentives for the development of small agribusiness firms managed by women; export crops specifically contracted out to women farmers; measures that provide child care for women who are agricultural wage laborers; and policies that assure access to credit. *Agricultural research* could improve food crops grown by women; develop food-processing and storage technologies for women farmers; investigate links between commodity improvement and better family nutrition; and produce ecologically sound farming and agroforestry techniques that utilize the knowledge of, or can be adapted by, women farmers.

50

Agricultural extension services should help raise the productivity of women-managed farms rather than provide courses in home economics and crafts, as many now do. Extension agents trained in a farming-systems approach and in crops that women grow could receive special incentives to work with women farmers. Communications techniques can easily reach illiterate or poorly educated women. Women's access to information can be improved by using existing networks of women's production teams and social groups. Information can be made available at places where they gather. Training does not necessarily require extensive time away from home or village. Farm-training centers can emphasize the training of couples and accommodate women farmers who are heads of households by providing training directly to them where they work.

Universities and vocational agricultural schools can actively recruit women for careers in agriculture and forestry. The number of women extensionists can be expanded and incorporated into mainstream activities of ministries, NGOs and rural cooperative federations on an equal basis with men. These women will not be effective, however, unless they are able to offer services or products that will yield material benefits.

To take on conservation work, women need secure legal rights to land. Donors need to pressure governments to grant these rights. NGOs and rural cooperative federations can help women negotiate titles or other permanent arrangements. Wherever possible, programs should link environmental improvements to income-earning opportunities. Food processing can be linked to food production.

Lastly, the job quality and working conditions of women who work in modern agribusinesses can be improved. Equal pay for equal work and training in new technologies that will enable them to do more than perform manual labor in the least remunerative jobs are long past due.

Credit

Credit is fundamental to improving women's standard of living. Providing women with access to credit requires policy, programmatic and legal changes. Reform of interest rate policies and provision of appropriate subsidies will probably be necessary but they are unlikely to be sufficient. Financial reforms need to be accompanied, or even preceded, by the development of equitable intermediary credit institutions with programs intended to "graduate" women into formal-sector borrowing. NGOs, cooperative federations and trade unions that already manage credit programs and provide technical assistance to borrowers are natural candidates to serve as intermediaries between basic credit needs and sophisticated credit requirements.

Legal reforms are also important. In many countries, women are still required to obtain permission to borrow, or obtain a financial guarantee, from husbands, brothers or fathers in order to qualify for loans. Successful credit programs for microenterprises and small businesses in which women predominate should be expanded and linked to formal-sector borrowing.

Formal-Sector Employment

Most women are still clustered in low-skill service or clerical jobs with little potential for advancement. In many developing countries young urban women who are semiskilled or unskilled find wage employment on assembly lines in local factories or multinational corporations that produce clothing and pharmaceuticals, process food or assemble electronics equipment.

Three views dominate opinions about employment by multinational firms in export-processing zones, such as that along the U.S.-Mexican border. One view holds that multinationals offer women employment opportunities they would not otherwise have, and better wages and working conditions than in domestic firms. When pressured by national governments, multinationals have been more willing than local industries to upgrade the work environment. An opposing view emphasizes the failure of multinationals to provide women with new options or long-term employment possibilities, stressing that corporations encourage turnover after a few years, accept a sexually segregated work force and paternalistic management practices, and pay women lower wages than men.

The third view holds that employment in export-processing zones can be less exploitative. Multinationals can pay women employees at least the minimum wage where it exists. Employers who provide more—transportation to and from factories; medical services that not only treat occupational illnesses and injuries but also provide primary health care, including family planning services; subsidized cafeterias to improve the nutrition and health of workers; child-care facilities on or off site; labor referral and preliminary training programs, and savings and loan plans to encourage women to save—are likely to have a more stable, better trained and more productive work force with a lower turnover rate. Lastly, such employers can supposedly tolerate workers' associations or trade unions more easily than smaller-size domestic employers.

Similar recommendations can be made for domestic industries. Demand for female labor in the formal sector needs to be expanded and governments can do so by promoting labor-intensive domestic as well as export industries, such as leather products, electrical appliances and food processing. Factory jobs should expand women's economic options rather than exploit them. A key factor is access to education and appropriate training.

Education

Education for women is both a development and an equity issue. The initial problem in women's education is getting girls into school and keeping them there. Low literacy levels of women go hand in hand with poverty and cultural mores, particularly in rural areas where low enrollment and high dropout rates result from the belief that it is more important to educate boys. In addition, some governments tend to give higher priority and more funds to secondary and higher education, leaving the initial imbalance between girls and boys unaddressed. Once in school, sexual segregation in curriculum and tracking prepare women for traditional female occupations. The problem of the "hidden curriculum" is common to both developed and developing countries.

The past 20 years have demonstrated that rapid expansion of education does not solve problems. Third World governments find themselves unable to create jobs for those currently educated. Expanding women's access in the face of massive unemployment and underemployment, cutbacks in education budgets and overwhelming debt burdens will not be easy. Investing in women's education, nonetheless, is a sound and cost-effective strategy. A growing body of evidence indicates that primary education and economic productivity result in lower birthrates, later marriages, improved family health and a dramatic decrease in infant mortality.

Policies that favor primary education, particularly in rural areas, bring long-term benefits. Incentives—such as scholarships or stipends to keep girls in school, locating schools close to homes in rural areas, building separate schools for girls and boys where culture dictates that the sexes not mingle, and transportation for girls—are useful initiatives. Classes held for short periods of time on a daily basis, rather than for longer periods at greater intervals, are likely to encourage attendance and still allow girls and women to continue productive activities. Flexible timing of both formal and nonformal education classes will also encourage attendance of women and girls. Girls who do go beyond primary school should be encouraged to choose nontraditional subjects, such as mathematics, science or agriculture. Finally, education

Training Women in Nontraditional Skills: Jamaica

The women's Construction Collective was established in Kingston, Jamaica, in 1983 to train and place unemployed women in jobs in the building and construction industry. Women are selected on the basis of personal recommendations as well as literacy and numeracy tests. They learn basic building skills and an understanding of construction terminology. In its first two and a half years, the collective trained 34 women and placed over 90 percent of them in construction jobs in plumbing, masonry, carpentry, electrical installation, painting and steelwork. The women earn $18 per week in contrast to the official weekly minimum wage of $10. More than 15 women have received additional training. Two women have completed the construction technology course at the College of Arts, Sciences and Technology, and two other women manage the collective. The collective has launched a repair and maintenance business, a carpentry workshop and, because construction workers must provide their own tools, a revolving fund to assist workers to purchase tools.

budgets should give priority to the education of women and girls. In times of scarce financial resources, the shifting of budget allocations to close the gap between females and males is a wise investment.

Training

Skills training for women is necessary to enable them to catch up with men and improve their employment options. Governments, NGOs and the private sector can all play a role. Training can be long-term, such as vocational education programs, or can consist of short courses. The best training programs are linked to production and in many cases offer literacy and numeracy, as well as agricultural, commercial or vocational skills. Vocational education programs are more likely to be part of the formal school system, but the private sector and NGOs are well suited to implement short courses. Vocational education schools should include women in training programs in nontraditional skills *for which there is a market*, such as plumbing, electrical wiring, construction or cabinetmaking. Short courses can focus on accounting and small-business skills and on improving the quality of goods produced by women entrepreneurs.

Health

The general health levels of women must be improved. Too many maternal/child health programs emphasize the child and ignore the mother. Too often women put the health of their children and their families first and do not seek medical attention until they are seriously ill. The health of women is directly linked to their productive capacity and their ability to care for their families. Women need increased access to health care.

The burdens of a double day (rural or urban workloads in addition to household responsibilities) place a heavy physical and mental strain on poor women of all ages. The unequal distribution of food within the family takes a heavy toll on girl children and their mothers, who are likely to be pregnant or nursing. Women are also predisposed to illnesses that are different in nature from those that affect men, such as those related to their reproductive roles. These include sexually transmitted diseases, the after-effects of clandestinely induced abortions, the physical toll of adolescent and repeated pregnancies, contraceptive side effects, malnutrition and anemia.

Assisting women farmers to grow more and better quality food crops and urban women microentrepreneurs to increase their incomes will improve the overall nutrition of women and children. These measures, combined with better primary health care, especially in rural areas, will lead to improved health. Programs should include not only immunizations, hygiene, sanitation, first aid and basic maternal/child care, but also reproductive health care: access to safe and effective contraception, treatment of sexually transmitted diseases and other gynecological problems, and care for complications arising from abortions. More effective distribution and greater availability of medicines and contraceptives and more flexible hours at clinics and health posts will increase women's access to them.

Health researchers should anticipate future problems involved in providing services to largely urban, predominantly female, aging populations. Ministries of health in developing countries will have to expand health delivery systems and develop community-based health services to meet demand.

Conclusion

Implementation of this agenda requires profound cultural and attitudinal changes within societies. Recognition of this truth has mobilized women activists in both industrialized and developing countries into an increasingly powerful force. Women have learned that the political will necessary for serious action by donor agencies and governments is contingent on women's organizing to pressure for change. The consensus women have reached has given them the strength to move into the mainstream. At the same time, shrinking national budgets do not bode well for the future. It seems likely that the degree of attention given to women's needs will depend on renewed interest in poverty alleviation, on the one hand, and on competing economic and political factors that may restrict or redirect public and development assistance, on the other. Targeting economic and other policies and resources to improve women's status and enhance their productive capacity, however, is essential to overcome the debt crisis and enable developing countries to move toward stable long-term growth. Without the full participation of women, poor countries will not be able to move beyond crisis and achieve sustainable economic progress in the next decades.

Talking It Over

A Note for Students and Discussion Groups

This issue of the HEADLINE SERIES, like its predecessors, is published for every serious reader, specialized or not, who takes an interest in the subject. Many of our readers will be in classrooms, seminars or community discussion groups. Particularly with them in mind, we present below some discussion questions—suggested as a starting point only—and references for further reading.

Discussion Questions

According to the authors, women are key to development. If so, why were their economic contributions overlooked for so long?

Women—as workers and home producers—have been undercounted in censuses. If you were collecting information on women's work, what questions would you ask of women to see how they contribute to economic growth?

Although many people and organizations have made a concerted effort to include women in development projects, not all efforts have been successful. What have some of the problems been in implementing and continuing projects? Why is the question of financial control so important (for both administrators and recipients)?

There is a debate over whether women's organizations are better able or less able to work with poor women in developing countries than other organizations. What do you see as the advantages—or disadvantages of women working with women?

In an international economy affected by the debt crisis, women carry an ever-greater burden of family responsibility and economic hardship. What are the areas for expansion and improvement that would most benefit women in employment, home production and family upkeep?

Poor women who work in the fields or market also care for children, the household, and husbands or male partners. This unpaid double day affects women's health and well-being. Suggest ideas to alleviate women's burden, or think of arguments to persuade men to share the household responsibilities. What are some of the obstacles you see to persuading men to share the work load? How would you present your arguments to a development planner? What are the obstacles you may run into when talking with him or her?

There is a link between women's advancement and social and economic progress. However, this is not apparent to everyone. Analyze why women receive less pay than men in the workplace. Why do you think women are willing to accept lower wages than men? Do you believe women are more responsible or less responsible in their work? Why?

If you had the opportunity (and the resources) to intervene in one sector of the economy to improve the situation of women, which one would you choose in order to have the most impact, and why?

Reading List

Boserup, Ester, *Women's Role in Economic Development*. New York, St. Martin's Press, 1974. An analysis of women's participation in the labor force in Africa, Asia and Latin America, under rural, urban and transitional economic labor systems. A classic on the subject of women in development.

Buvinić, Mayra, "Projects for Women in the Third World: Explaining Their Misbehavior." *World Development,* Vol. 14, No. 5, 1986. Relegating women to traditional roles as caretakers can deter their potential for income-generating projects.

———, and Lycette, Margaret, "Women, Poverty, and Development in the Third World." In *Strengthening the Poor: What Have We Learned?* edited by John Lewis. Washington, D.C., Overseas Development Council, 1988. Explains the need to look at women as gainful producers, especially in agriculture.

Dankelman, Irene, and Davidson, Joan, *Women and Environment in the Third World*. London, Earthscan Publications Limited, 1988. Analysis of women's role in the struggle to balance human needs and environmental concerns. Authors question the lack of resources available to meet this challenge.

Dauber, Roslyn, and Cain, Melinda L., eds., *Women and Technological Change in Developing Countries*. Boulder, Colo., Westview Press, 1981. Articles focus on the interrelationship between women and technology. If technology is to advance social and economic development, then women's control over and access to it is vital.

Dwyer, Daisy, and Bruce, Judith, eds., *A Home Divided: Women and Income in the Third World*. Stanford, Calif., Stanford University Press, 1988. Numerous authors look at the distribution of work and benefits within households for men and women, young and old.

Fraser, Arvonne S., *The UN Decade for Women: Documents and Dialogue.* Boulder, Colo., Westview Press, 1987. Ms. Fraser, senior fellow at the Hubert Humphrey Institute of Public Affairs, has condensed the four major documents of the UN Decade for Women.

Joekes, Susan, *Women in the World Economy.* New York, Oxford University Press, 1987. Prepared for the United Nations International Research and Training Institute for the Advancement of Women. The book measures women's economic contributions to devclopment through available statistics worldwide.

Leslie, Joanne, Lycette, Margaret, and Buvinić, Mayra, "Weathering Economic Crisis: The Crucial Role of Women in Health." In *Health, Nutrition, and Economic Crisis: Approaches to Policy in the Third World,* edited by David E. Bell and Michael R. Reich. Dover, Mass., Auburn House Publishing Co., 1988. This synopsis of a presentation at the Takemi Symposium on International Health in 1986 reflects a growing concern about the role of women in family health.

Nash, June, and Fernandez-Kelly, Maria Patricia, eds., *Women, Men, und the International Division of Labor.* Albany, N.Y., State University of New York Press, 1983. The major shifts in production in the past 30 years have allected economic and social relations and exacerbated the inequalities between women and men, minorities, and dominant racial and ethnic groups.

Seager, Joni, *Women in the World.* New York, Simon and Schuster, 1986. Maps, graphs and tables on health care, population, employment and education provide data on women around the world.

SEEDS. A pamphlet series edited by Kristin Anderson, et al. Available from P.O. Box 3923, Grand Central Station, New York, N.Y. 10163. The pamphlets describe income-generating projects developed by and for low-income women, in which women play decisionmaking roles.

Sen, Gita, and Grown, Caren, *Development, Crises, and Alternative Visions: Third World Women's Perspectives.* New York, Monthly Review Press, 1987. A thoughtful presentation by the Third World women's organization DAWN (Development Alternatives with

Women for a New Era), which summarizes the failures, successes, and lessons learned during the UN Decade for Women.

Sivard, Ruth Leger, *Women. . . . A World Survey.* Washington, D.C., World Priorities, 1985. International statistics provide a clear picture of women's disproportionate representation among the poor, the illiterate, the unemployed and underemployed, and the politically powerless.

Yudelman, Sally W., *Hopeful Openings: A Study of Five Women's Development Organizations in Latin America and the Caribbean.* West Hartford, Conn., Kumarian Press, 1987. An analysis of five organizations geared to the needs of women in Latin America and the Caribbean.

GLOSSARY OF INTERNATIONAL AID AGENCIES

United Nations Agencies Providing Assistance to Women in Development

Food and Agriculture Organization	FAO
International Labor Organization	ILO
International Research and Training Institute for the Advancement of Women	INSTRAW
UN Children's Fund	UNICEF
UN Development Fund for Women	UNIFEM
UN Development Program	UNDP
UN Economic Commission for Africa	ECA
UN Economic Commission for Latin America and the Caribbean	ECLAC
UN Economic and Social Commission for Asia and the Pacific	ESCAP
UN Fund for Population Activities	UNFPA
World Health Organization	WHO

Regional Organizations

European Economic Community	EEC
Organization of American States	OAS
South Asian Association for Regional Cooperation	SAARC
Southern African Development Coordination Conference	SADCC

Bilateral Agencies Providing International Development Assistance

Australia	Australian International Development Assistance Bureau
Britain	Overseas Development Administration (ODA)
Canada	Canadian International Development Agency (CIDA)
	International Development Research Center (IDRC)
Denmark	Danish International Development Agency (DANIDA)
Finland	Ministry for Foreign Affairs, Department for International Development Cooperation
France	Ministry of Cooperation for International Development
Italy	Directorate General for Development Cooperation, Ministry of Foreign Affairs
Japan	Policy Coordination Division, Economic Cooperation Bureau, Ministry of Foreign Affairs

Netherlands	Ministry of Foreign Affairs, Directorate General for International Cooperation
Norway	Norwegian Agency for Development
Spain	Agency of Cooperation, Ministry of Foreign Affairs
Sweden	Swedish International Development Agency (SIDA)
Switzerland	Directorate for Development and Humanitarian Aid, Ministry of Foreign Affairs
United States	African Development Foundation
	Agency for International Development (AID)
	Inter-American Foundation (IAF)
West Germany	Federal Ministry for Economic Cooperation

International Financial Institutions

African Development Bank (AfDB)

Asian Development Bank (ADB)

Inter-American Development Bank (IADB)

International Monetary Fund (IMF)

World Bank (International Bank for Reconstruction and Development, IBRD)

This issue of the HEADLINE SERIES has been made possible by the generosity of Avon Products, Inc. and the Rockefeller Foundation.